Stop Smoking

The Authentic Account Of An Individual With A Persistent Smoking Habit Who Successfully Overcame The Addiction Without Experiencing Any Withdrawal Symptoms

(Including Why I Started Smoking And How I Broke Free Of My Habit)

Dr. Wade Chambers

TABLE OF CONTENT

Introduction 1

Acquiring An Awareness Of The Dangers Of Smoking 8

Getting Ready To Call It Quits 15

Lifestyle Changes 19

How To Adjust It So That It Fits Your Requirements 35

The Arguments In Favor Of Quitting 56

Alterations To One's Way Of Life In Order To Facilitate Quitting 61

Strategies For Physical Withdrawal Are Presented In An Attempt To Help Users Kick Their Habits 68

Signs And Symptoms Of Withdrawal 75

What Makes You Wish To Give Up Smoking? .. 79

Creating A Robust Support Network 87

Recognizing The Connection Between Smoking And Reducing Stress 108

Exploring The Addictive Nature Of Nicotine 112

Sustaining An Alcohol-Free Lifestyle 118

Why Is It So Hard For Me To Stop Smoking? 127

Locating Help And Encouragement Along Your Path To Quitting 131

The Complete And Final List Of Excuses To Give Up On Something 140

The Arguments In Favor Of Quitting 150

There Are Numerous Varieties Of Smoking Products 161

Words Have Power: How Hypnotic Suggestions Can Change Habits [The Power Of Words] ... 169

Introduction

A strong-willed young man by the name of Max lived in a cozy little suburb that was tucked away among the gently undulating hills. It was common knowledge that Max had been battling an unhealthy habit for quite some time: smoking. But at some point, he made the decision to escape the stranglehold it had on him.

Max set out to find a support group that specialized in assisting persons in kicking their smoking habit with unyielding determination. There, he found kindred spirits who knew the hardships he was going through and provided advise that was really helpful. Max set out on a path toward self-discovery and rehabilitation, bolstered by the unfailing support of his friends and family.

He gradually gave up smoking in favor of more physically and mentally beneficial activities like exercise and meditation. He removed himself from settings that could have triggered his anxiety and surrounded himself with supportive people and influences. Max would remind himself of his goals, ambitions, and the future that he envisioned for himself whenever he started to experience cravings.

After a number of months, Max reached a major milestone: he had successfully abstained from smoking for an entire year. Because of the victory, he now possesses a revitalized feeling of self-assurance and resiliency. Max became an example for everyone around him by telling his experience and urging others to follow in his footsteps and find their own way to freedom.

Max demonstrated to the entire globe that it is possible to break free from addiction by sheer perseverance and the help of a community that is supportive.

WHY IT IS IMPORTANT THAT ADOLescentS SHOULD NOT SMOKE

Impact Unfavorable on the Growth of the Lungs: The development of the lungs is most important during the adolescent years. When a person smokes, dangerous chemicals and poisons are breathed into their lungs, which hinders the growth and function of the lungs. This can result in a decreased lung capacity, an increased risk of developing respiratory infections, and ongoing respiratory problems.

Increased Potential for Addictive Behavior: Nicotine addiction is more likely to develop in young people than it is in adults. The brain of a developing adolescent is particularly susceptible to the addictive properties of nicotine, which can result in a dependency on cigarettes or other tobacco products that lasts a person's entire life.

Damage to Brain Development Research has shown that youths who use tobacco have impaired brain development. Memory and attention span can both suffer as a result of its negative effects on cognitive function, which include disrupting the creation of neural connections. This may have repercussions that last a very long time for academic performance as well as general intellectual development.

Increased Probability of Substance Abuse Smoking during adolescence is associated with an increased likelihood of engaging in other dangerous behaviors, including alcohol and drug abuse. Smoking makes it more likely that a person will become addicted to more than one substance since it is a gateway drug that leads to experimentation with other substances.

A Significant Raising of the Risk of Numerous Health Issues Smoking during adolescence considerably enhances the risk of a wide variety of health issues, both in the short term and in the long term. These conditions include respiratory diseases, cardiovascular disorders, cancer (especially lung cancer), compromised immune systems, and different oral health difficulties such as gum disease and tooth loss. Lung cancer is the most common form of cancer.

Impact on society and the mind The habit of smoking can have a detrimental effect on one's ability to interact with others and their sense of self-worth. Teens who smoke may be subjected to stigma, exclusion, and disapproval from their peers, which can result in feelings of isolation and a reduction in the number of possibilities to participate in social activities. Inability to quit smoking can also contribute to emotions of guilt and humiliation, as well as a diminished sense of one's own value.

A burden on one's finances, smoking is an expensive habit that can quickly deplete the available financial resources of a youngster. The money that is spent on cigarettes could be better invested in satisfying other need or desires, such as education, hobbies, or long-term objectives.

It is essential for adolescents to have this knowledge in order for them to make educated decisions regarding their own health. It is possible to prevent and reduce teenage smoking by educating young people about the dangers of smoking, fostering surroundings that are tobacco-free, and providing access to support networks. This will protect the health of the teenagers as well as their future opportunities.

Acquiring An Awareness Of The Dangers Of Smoking

The act of lighting and inhaling smoke from the combustion of a material, most commonly tobacco, is referred to as smoking. Nicotine, tar, carbon monoxide, and a variety of other cancer-causing agents are only some of the toxic substances that are present in cigarette smoke.

Tobacco smoking is a significant contributor to a number of different health conditions, the most notable of which are lung cancer, chronic obstructive pulmonary disease (COPD), heart disease, and respiratory infections. In addition to the fact that it is harmful to the body in a physical sense, smoking also has the potential to be addicting and difficult to quit.

Cancer of the lung Smoking is the primary factor responsible for lung cancer, which is the most prevalent form of the disease throughout the world.

Chronic obstructive pulmonary disease, sometimes known as COPD, is a term that refers to a set of lung disorders that can make it difficult to breathe. COPD is almost often caused by the habit of smoking.

Heart disease: Smoking causes damage to the blood vessels and raises the risk of developing heart disease, which in turn increases the risk of having a heart attack, a stroke, or other cardiovascular disorders.

Infections of the respiratory system Smoking lowers the body's resistance to infection and makes it harder for the immune system to do its job, both of which contribute to an increased likelihood of contracting respiratory infections such as pneumonia and bronchitis.

Reduced fertility: Both men and women who smoke have a greater risk of experiencing reduced fertility, which makes it more challenging to conceive.

Early aging: Smoking can hasten the aging process, resulting in wrinkles and other forms of skin damage that appear earlier than they otherwise would.

Oral health issues Smoking can lead to a number of oral health issues, the most common of which are periodontal disease, tooth decay, and oral cancer.

Increased risk of other cancers Smoking is linked to a higher chance of developing a variety of other cancers, including those of the bladder, cervix, esophagus, kidney, liver, pancreas, and stomach.

Listed below are some concrete examples of how smoking might negatively affect your health:

Tobacco use is the leading cause of death from lung cancer, accounting for around 80 percent of all cases. The risk of developing lung cancer in smokers is anywhere from 15 to 30 times higher than in non-smokers.

Smoking is the leading contributor to chronic obstructive pulmonary disease (COPD), which includes emphysema and chronic bronchitis. COPD is known to induce a variety of respiratory symptoms, including wheezing, chronic coughing, and shortness of breath.

Diseases of the heart Smoking causes damage to the blood vessels and raises the chance of developing cardiovascular diseases. Smokers have a 2 to 4 times increased risk of developing heart disease compared to people who do not smoke.

Infections of the respiratory system Smoking lowers the immune system's defenses, making it more difficult for the body to fend off infections, particularly those that affect the respiratory system. People who smoke have a significantly increased risk of developing respiratory infections such as bronchitis and pneumonia.

Reduced fertility is one of the potential side effects of smoking, which can affect both men and women. Women who smoke have a more difficult time conceiving a child, while males whose fertility is affected by smoking have lower sperm counts.

Early aging: Smoking can hasten the aging process, leading to wrinkles, poor skin, and other telltale indicators of aging that appear earlier than they should.

Oral health issues Smoking can lead to a number of oral health issues, the most common of which are periodontal disease, tooth decay, and oral cancer.

Increased risk of other cancers Smoking is linked to a higher chance of developing a variety of other cancers, including those of the bladder, cervix, esophagus, kidney, liver, pancreas, and stomach.

These are just some of the many negative effects that smoking can have on your health. If you are a smoker and want to lower your risk of acquiring these and other health problems, as well as enhance your general health and well-being, you should consider quitting smoking.

Getting Ready To Call It Quits

Quitting smoking has many positive effects, both physically and mentally, on a person's health.

1. Improved lung function Quitting smoking can improve lung function and reduce the risk of developing lung diseases such as chronic obstructive pulmonary disease (also known as COPD) and lung cancer.

2. Improved health of the arteries Smoking increases the risk of developing cardiovascular disease, stroke, and high blood pressure. Giving up smoking is one way to enhance one's circulatory health and reduce the risk of developing certain diseases.

3. greater energy and stamina: Putting an end to a smoking habit can result in greater energy and stamina, which can make it simpler to carry out activities that require physical exertion.

4. An improved state of mind Smoking is associated with significantly increased levels of worry, depression, and stress. Quitting smoking is associated with improvements in mental health as well as overall well-being.

In order to keep oneself enthused throughout the process of quitting smoking, it is vital to keep one's mind on the positive aspects of quitting, including the changes in one's sound. Here are some suggestions for maintaining your drive:

1. Jot down the advantages of quitting: Writing out the advantages of quitting

will help people remember why it is so important to stop smoking and keep people motivated to do so.

2. Look for Support Seeking support, whether it be from friends, family, or a support group, can assist individuals in maintaining their motivation and sense of responsibility while they are in the process of buying.

3. Commemorate significant achievements: Commemorating significant achievements, such as going a week or a month without smoking, can assist people in maintaining their motivation and making them feel pleased of their success.

4. Engage in activities that promote self-care: Engaging in activities that promote self-care, such as exercise, meditation, or spending time outdoors, can help relieve

stress and increase well-being, making it easier to stay inspired and focused on stopping, which will make it easier for you to stop smoking.

Lifestyle Changes

A healthy lifestyle that supports your goal of being smoke-free should be adopted when you quit smoking since quitting smoking is about more than just giving up smokes on their own. Modifications to one's way of life have a key role in breaking the cycle of addiction and establishing the foundation for sustained sobriety. In this piece, we talk about the relevance of making changes to your lifestyle and how they could be able to help you on your journey to a life free of smoking.

Reconstruct Your Daily Habits

Making improvements to your lifestyle will need you to reevaluate and adjust your typical activities. Making deliberate adjustments could assist you in developing new habits that do not involve smoking. This is due to the fact that smoking is generally associated with particular activities or triggers.

The Process of Identifying Triggers

Understanding the factors that cause you to smoke is essential to making lifestyle changes that will last. Is it the pressure, the social gatherings, or certain times of the day? If you are able to identify your triggers, you will have a better chance of finding healthier alternatives to deal with them.

A Diet and Nutrition That Is Healthy

The adoption of a diet rich in nutrients not only improves your overall health but also has the potential to assist in the management of cravings. Make sure that the majority of your meals consist of lean proteins, fruits and vegetables, whole grains, and healthy fats. Keeping yourself hydrated with water and herbal teas can also help prevent cravings for unhealthy foods.

Frequent physical activity

Exercising your muscles offers a plethora of benefits, including the reduction of stress, improvement of your mood, and expansion of your lung capacity. Take part in activities that interest you, such as walking, cycling, or yoga, for example. Not only does physical activity divert your attention away from desires, but it also improves your overall health.

How to Deal with Stress One of the main reasons people smoke is stress. It's possible that better ways to cope with stress, such deep breathing, meditation, or journaling, can be found through learning stress management strategies like these, which can also help reduce the temptation to smoke.

Developing Areas That Are Smoke-Free

Make all of your indoor spaces, including your living quarters and your place of business, smoke-free zones. You should thoroughly clean your home to get rid of the odor of smoke, and you should also consider moving furniture around to break any links that may exist with smoking areas.

Social Group That Is There To Offer Support

Put yourself in an environment where you are surrounded by family and friends who will encourage you and respect your decision to quit smoking. Participate in social activities that do not center on smoking, and look for companionship that aligns with your goals of quitting smoking.

New pastimes and pursuits to engage in

Focus your work on developing new skills and interests that capture your interest. Pursuing activities in the arts, on the athletic field, or in the classroom can help keep your mind active and give you a sense of accomplishment.

Meditation and taking care of oneself

Maintaining awareness of your feelings and state of health can be accomplished through the practice of mindfulness and self-care. You may find that cultivating mindful awareness helps you manage cravings and prevents relapse. Make getting enough rest, relaxing, and engaging in activities that offer you joy your top priorities.

Modifications to your way of life are an essential component of any effort to give up smoking. Not only will you be able to break free from nicotine addiction, but you will also be establishing the groundwork for long-term health and happiness by addressing the triggers that led to your addiction, adopting healthy behaviors, and cultivating an environment that is supportive. Keep in mind that each positive change you make contributes to your success and boosts your commitment to live a life free from the effects of smoking.

The Process of Recognizing Habits and Triggers

In order to successfully quit smoking, one of the most important steps is to recognize the habits and behaviors that are linked to the habit. Recognizing these inclinations enables you to develop strategies for overcoming cravings to smoke and substituting it with activities that are less harmful to your health. In this article, we delve into the relevance of understanding triggers and patterns, and we investigate how choosing healthier alternatives may help pave the route toward a life free from smoking.

Gaining an Understanding of Habits and Triggers

The conditions, sensations, or cues that cause one to have the want to smoke are referred to as triggers. On the other hand, habits are defined as acts that are performed repeatedly and are associated with smoking. It is essential to interrupt the cycle of smoking addiction to first identify the triggers, and then establish new routines.

Awareness of Oneself

Having a strong sense of self-awareness is essential to being able to identify habits and triggers. Take note of the situations in which you have the strongest need to smoke. Is it after eating, when you're in a stressful situation, or when you're hanging out with a certain group of people? Keeping an eye out for these patterns can assist you in identifying your triggers.

Keeping a Journal of Your Triggers

Keeping a journal or diary could prove to be quite beneficial. Record in a journal every instance in which you are overcome with a need to smoke and make a note of the circumstances and emotions that accompany the urge. Over the course of time, patterns will emerge, providing you with an understanding of your triggers.

Investigating Various Alternative Courses of Action

After you've recognized your triggers and patterns, it's time to start looking into non-tobacco options that are better for your health. These choices provide helpful ways to respond to stressful situations without resorting to unhealthy behaviors like smoking.

As someone who works in the fitness industry as a coach and trainer, I've always been interested in the subject of habits and changes, which is why I decided to tackle the issue of smoking addiction. My battle with smoking was difficult but ultimately victorious, and as a result, I came to the conclusion that smoking is not a dumb habit; rather, it is one that should be started. Tobacco use is a serious problem and a true addiction.

The initial stages

I worked as a trainer for a company that was in the sales industry about fifteen years ago. My responsibilities included staff training, personnel management, and skill development. In a nutshell, I monitored the progress that my coworkers made in their own personal and professional lives, which was an important factor in the expansion of the company. What exactly does this discussion have to do with assisting people in giving up smoking? It is related to the degree to which it was my responsibility to encourage individuals to get better, make changes, and accomplish their objectives. In order to perform my job more effectively, I needed to convince and motivate both customers and coworkers. And I can say that my achievement brought me a lot of joy. To the point where I occasionally brought about, in a manner that was not quite conscious, or rather, without having determined beforehand, a significant shift in their behavior and in their lives. I became aware that I was able to "manipulate" certain circumstances in order to bring about a change in a person in a relatively short amount of time. After a few months had passed after he had stopped smoking, a coworker with whom I was in close touch at the time disclosed to me that it was I, who "triggered the click" and pushed him to stop smoking during a meeting. He told me this after he had been smoke-free for a few months. After inadvertently assisting one of my coworkers in leaving, I continued working with a large number of other colleagues. I came to the conclusion that "smoking" was not a topic that should be treated flippantly. The tragedy of this addiction was something I had either grossly underestimated or never given sufficient thought to. Before that, I had the impression that smokers were just plain ignorant. This is not how it happened. I found myself confronted with the most destructive addiction of our time, and possibly of all time. I recall that one day I walked into a pub to get some coffee, and while I was there I started a conversation with the folks who were there about cigarettes, which was a topic that had recently started to fascinate me. When discussing the negative effects of smoking, I brought up the fact that cigarettes are also a contributor to impotence in people. In that situation, a woman who was considered to be at the very least "gallant" felt the need to defend the category by claiming that her sexual encounters with smokers had always been great. She said that she felt forced to do so. I will not tell you how insignificant I felt; I really wanted to vanish. But it was helpful for me to realize that the smoker has the urge - I would say a physiological need - to defend smoking even more than they have the need to smoke cigarettes themselves. To this day, I have never come into such resistance, which can be comparable to the one that smokers experience. Any other individual who is addicted to substance usage will typically have a sense of personal and social difficulties, such as the admission of being a prisoner of their substance of choice, unable to function normally without their substance of choice, and declaration of addiction to their substance of choice.

On the other hand, the smoker does not give up smoking because he does not view the issue with cigarettes as having the same level of significance.

A fresh obstacle on both the personal and professional fronts

Up until that point, I had never given any thought to leveraging what I did and what I know to assist others in giving up their smoking habit. However, the primary focus remained on assisting the development of others. As a result, I decided to play a "game" to help my smoking pals kick the habit, and it turned out to be successful! "If it works, and then they are fine thanks to you," I told myself, "do it!" As a result, I started looking into the topic more and learning more about the different communication and coaching tactics that are associated with smoking. Each and every day, I put the smoker's persuasion to work on anyone I came into contact with. "Because-I-like" has always been my go-to choice of justification. The "I will never stop" refrain also counts. I put my strategies to use without charge and worked to improve them over time. I prepared myself by studying, and then I applied. I encouraged and influenced them to give up smoking. Sixty-eight percent of the folks who came to see me were able to kick the habit of smoking in a relatively short amount of time. Some of them within the hour, after only one appointment (they most definitely put my advice into practice even later). Others did so in a few weeks, while others still needed a few months to complete it. Only 35% of them had gone back to smoking within the first year after quitting, which is why new meetings were required. However, of the latter group, only fifty percent had resumed their previous level of cigarette consumption, while the remainder "smoked" (to quote one of them) no more than a handful of cigarettes on a daily basis.

How To Adjust It So That It Fits Your Requirements

You are now aware of the strategy that I ultimately employed to break free from the shackles of my smoking habit. I am confident that you will acknowledge that it is simple and uncomplicated. It's possible that it's not the quickest solution, but as we've established, you didn't start smoking in a day, so breaking the habit shouldn't happen all at once either, if you want the simplest and most effective outcomes. As a result of the fact that I stumbled into the technique by accident, I was unable to comprehend it at first, which is why it took me a very long time to finally kick my smoking habit. I took too much time in several steps, and I dragged out the smoking of the final cigarette for much longer than was necessary or prudent. You can avoid this by engaging in the necessary planning and self-control. If I were to do it all over again with the information that I have today, the first stage would be to manage jumps of two hours every two weeks. The final step would be to smoke one cigarette every day for one week, and then that would be it. I will see you again. I think it's safe to state that at this point. I am aware that there were times when I struggled, but I made it through, and you can too.

During the first two weeks after quitting smoking, I would have my first cigarette at ten in the morning. Following that, I would switch to the noon shift for another two weeks, and so on. I would not disclose my plans to anyone and would not discuss them with anyone else. In my experience, the less words that are used, the better. Let my deeds speak for themselves, but this is the approach that has been successful for me. You, on the other hand, could be unique and benefit much from the encouragement of others. If you have a friend who is also trying to kick the habit of smoking, you might find it helpful to go through this exercise together. You could encourage one another to keep going even when things are tough for either of you and support each other get through challenging moments. You are the only one who can determine what the most beneficial next step is for you. We are all unique individuals.

Create a strategy that caters to your requirements and write it down. If you feel that jumping for two hours at a time is too much for you, try jumping for one hour at a time instead. If you find that two weeks for each phase is not sufficient, take three. You act in accordance with what seems appropriate to you. Having said that, you shouldn't deviate from your intended schedule after you've already created it. Put your name on it, and proceed with full assurance. You have the ability to succeed. As soon as you have your strategy written down, you should display it in a place where it can be observed, and then you should get started. Establish a beginning time, and then get to work.

If you smoke 28 cigarettes every day from eight in the morning until ten at night, here's what your schedule may look like:

StepWhen does smoking each day begin?Beginning of the period: daily consumption of smokesCheck the box once the goal is reached.

You at the moment8 am on the thirty first of June 28 1 10 am on the first of July 24 2 12 pm3.2 o'clock on the 14th of Julythe 28th of July at 16:40:00 pm11th of August 12:00 PM 5:00 PM 6:00 PMthe 25th of August from 6:00 to 8:00 pmSeptember 8th, between 4 and 7 and 9 o'clockthe 22nd day of September 1 8Completed on the 6th of OctoberCongratulations, you've reached your goal!

As you start your trip, you could experience fleeting cravings every now and again that last for little longer than a minute and a half. When you feel them coming on, redirect your thoughts to something that will make you feel better; for instance, instead of thinking about smoking, think about the vacation you are going to organize. I strongly suggest that you always carry a bottle of water with you since drinking it is an excellent way to satisfy a craving, and I urge that you always have a bottle of water with you. However, once you get into the zone, I think you will be astonished at how simple this will be for you to accomplish.

Evenings were always a particularly challenging time for me. After a long day at work, I would either watch television or head to my neighborhood watering hole for a couple pints of beer. These were the smokes that I enjoyed the most and I always felt like I deserved them at the end of a long and trying day, as if they were some kind of reward. However, I was aware that they were not and that it was necessary for them to be eliminated. When the time came to get rid of them, I began going for walks in the evening every day. This helped divert me, and it was extremely refreshing because it gave me much more life to devote to active pursuits after I had completed it. I always had a bottle of water with me, and whenever I got the need to smoke, I would take a swig from the water instead. This turned out quite well. When it came time for the final step, I decided to continue smoking one cigarette per day for a considerable amount of time. Although many people could benefit from this, there is a risk associated with it. As is common knowledge, you run the risk of falling back into your former smoking routine because this is how the smoking trap operates. You cannot credibly claim to be a non-smoker if you smoke even one cigarette per day. If so, how? Saying that you don't smoke gives you a certain amount of authority. It bolsters your belief, which in turn will assist you in staying away from them. My recommendation is that you finish the last cigarette quickly and move on. Put an end to it as quickly as you can.

I do a lot of fishing, and in order to get to my favorite site, which is at the bottom of a very high cliff, I have to climb down. It is not difficult to descend, but it is quite difficult to get back up again. Due to the fact that I am a smoker, I was only able to climb one portion at a time since I needed to stop and catch my breath at regular intervals. Due to the fact that it was such a frustrating experience, I generally avoided going fishing there because it wasn't worth the trouble. My efforts to cut back on smoking coincided with an increase in my ability to scale this cliff, which was first quite difficult. This was a terrific sign of how well I was doing and how my smoking habits were genuinely limiting me in my ability to do certain things. After a period of eight years, I am now able to deal with it without becoming anxious or needing a break. I simply aim upwards and fire away without giving it any attention. This is one of the many benefits of giving up smoking.

Getting Ready for Your Quit Date, Recognizing Your Triggers, and Establishing Your Quit Date are the Topics Covered in Chapter 3.

The Process of Identifying Triggers

Making the decision to quit smoking is a respectable one that has the potential to dramatically improve one's quality of life as well as one's health. The process of recognizing the triggers that are responsible for your smoking habit is one of the most important components of this procedure. Your chances of successfully quitting smoking can be significantly improved if you take the time to become aware of and address these triggers. In this piece, we will discuss the significance of recognizing triggers, as well as the most efficient ways to get ready for the day you decide to quit smoking.

Why It Is Important to Identifying Triggers

The situations, emotions, or circumstances that set off your craving for cigarettes are referred to as triggers. There is a possibility that both internal variables (psychological or emotional) and external elements (environmental or social) are at play here. It is critical that you have a solid understanding of these triggers because it enables you to develop coping methods to deal with them without resorting to smoking.

Actions to Take in Order to Pinpoint Triggers

Reflection Upon Oneself: Your smoking habits should be the first thing you consider. When and where do you usually light up a cigarette? Do you find that certain emotions make you want to smoke more than others? Understanding your habits may make it simpler for you to identify the things that set you off.

Maintain a Journal: Keep a journal for a period of one to two weeks before the date you aim to quit smoking. Maintain a log of every time you light up, noting the specifics of the situation. Were you tense, did you have nothing to do, or were you with friends? Using this notepad to help you identify your triggers may make the process much simpler.

Try to Find Help: Talk to loved ones who have successfully kicked the habit of smoking and ask for their encouragement and support. They might be able to share information on the triggers that they experienced and the ways that they overcame them. Having support from other people who are going through the same thing can be quite helpful.

Help from Qualified Individuals: Consider having a conversation with a therapist or counselor who specializes in assisting individuals in kicking their smoking habit. They might be able to provide you with expert guidance on how to identify and manage your triggers. In addition to this, they could suggest particular procedures or treatments that are tailored to your need.

Common Triggers That Get People to Smoke

It could be helpful to begin by first gaining an awareness of the typical smoking triggers. Typical reasons consist of things like:

Under pressure: Many people use smoking as a method of self-care and relief from stressful situations. Find healthy ways to relieve stress other than smoking, such as meditation, exercise, or deep breathing, and give up the habit if you want to stay healthy.

Contexts of Human Interaction: Being around people who smoke, whether they are friends or coworkers, can be a powerful trigger. Share with them your intention to quit smoking, and ask for their support in avoiding the temptation to hand you a cigarette or other kind of tobacco.

Smoking as a Regular Habit: Certain routines that people engage in on a daily basis, such as smoking a cigarette with their morning coffee, have the potential to operate as powerful triggers. If you wish to get rid of these links, you'll need to change your routines.

Feelings : It's possible that anger, sorrow, or worry will make you desire to light up a cigarette. Acquire a variety of coping strategies for dealing with these feelings, such as having a conversation with a friend or participating in relaxation activities.

STEPS I TOOK THAT LED TO MY DECISION TO CANCEL MY SMOKING ADDICTION

sincerely commit to putting a stop to it.

According to research, those who try to quit smoking by gradually reducing the number of cigarettes they smoke each day have a lower chance of success than those who try to quit smoking by quitting cold turkey entirely. In the event that you just attempt to cut back, it is obvious that you will inhale more deeply and more frequently while you smoke in order to acquire the same amount of nicotine as you did in the past. As a result, when your quit date finally arrives, you absolutely must refrain from having even a single puff of a cigarette.

You could give up smoking right now, but doing so wouldn't give you much time to make preparations. According to the findings of numerous studies, genuine preparation will improve your chances of avoiding the use of tobacco products. The majority of people require a period of time comparable to several weeks in order to make all of their preparations. Your target stop date, if everything goes according to plan, shouldn't be subject to any considerable amount of stress. Choose a day within the next fourteen days when you will have the least access to the items that stimulate your want to smoke and make that the day you decide to quit smoking. Take a day off from work as an example and use that as your date to quit smoking.

Then make a commitment to yourself not to smoke after that date. You might demonstrate how seriously you take your responsibilities by bringing up the fact that you required a day in which everything operates as it should.

According to a number of studies, having support from family and friends might make it much simpler to give up smoking. It is a good idea to make this request for assistance before you actually give up. Do not, under any circumstances, be reluctant to talk with other people about how you are now feeling. Make sure that people are aware of the reasons why you need to stop smoking as well as how important it is for you to be successful. Inform them of what they can do best to assist you. In point of fact, even your friends who continue to smoke can be of assistance if they refrain from smoking in your presence and do not offer you smokes. You will find it easier to live a life free of tobacco if you have guidance and support to help you through the transition. Your primary care provider can provide you with helpful direction, but you can also benefit from participating in a group smoking cessation program. Research demonstrates that the more seriously you guide yourself, the greater your chances are of successfully quitting smoking.

Acquire New Capabilities and Behavior Patterns to Use Check out both the Pressure and the Feelings. When you make even minor adjustments to the routines you follow every day, you introduce a modicum of additional stress into your life. In spite of the fact that it's a noteworthy improvement, quitting smoking is not an exceptional circumstance. If you have a habit of smoking cigarettes as a way to relax whenever things get stressful, you may find that you are under a greater amount of strain than usual. When you feed your body nicotine, smoking gives you the illusion that you are more relaxed than you actually are. In any event, nicotine is a stimulant that speeds up the metabolism. Instead of relaxing your body, it actually speeds up your heart rate, increases the tightness in your blood vessels, and boosts your adrenaline level. There are many effective methods available for managing stress that do not involve the use of nicotine. Alter your routines and find something else to occupy your time. Altering your daily routines should be one of the first things you do when you decide to stop smoking. Take as an example attempting to drive a different route to work or substituting tea for espresso as your morning beverage. Distract yourself from the want to smoke by engaging in conversation with a friend or getting started on a new project.

Maintain a Dynamic Attitude: Active labor is an excellent strategy for delivering pressure, overcoming smoking urges, and alleviating the uncomfortable side effects of nicotine withdrawal. In addition to this, it acts to improve your physical health. If you are consistent with your practice, you will notice improvements in both how you appear and how you feel. This could provide you with further assurance in your decision to give up smoking. Active work doesn't necessarily need to be taxing in order to fulfill its accommodating function. If you have been a heavy smoker or if you have any illness for which you are receiving therapeutic care, it is possible that beginning a strenuous activity program is not safe for you. This is especially true if you have been a smoker for a long time. Gather some information to help you determine the appropriate level of action for you. Strolling is one of the most effective forms of exercise that almost everyone can do. Start off by strolling short distances at a slow pace, and then gradually pick up your pace as you become further apart. Make an effort to loosen up. Pleasantly relaxing Focus your attention on how you can relax whenever you become aware that you are beginning to experience tension. Take a step back with each breath. While you breathe in through your nose, softly repeat to yourself, "I am." While you exhale gradually from your mouth, quietly offer the signal "loose." As you continue to do this, you will find that you have a greater sense of freedom.

Give Yourself a Treat. Quitting smoking comes with its own set of rewards. For example: • It improves your health. • It enhances your ability to perceive the flavor and aroma of food. On the other hand, you won't be able to reap these benefits right away if you quit smoking. It is a good idea to convince yourself to quit smoking by creating a plan that includes immediate benefits as a reward for kicking the habit. For example: * Treat yourself to something you've been wanting all along or something you absolutely require.

• Go out for supper. • See a movie with a friend. • Do both of these things.

Spend some time right now making a list of rewards for yourself that you can enjoy once you have successfully quit smoking for at least two months.

The Arguments In Favor Of Quitting

In the United States, smoking is a significant problem that affects the public's health. A recent research from the Centers for Disease Control and Prevention found that more than 20% of adults in the United States smoke cigarettes, and of those individuals, more than 80% smoke cigarettes on a daily basis. An addiction to nicotine can result in a number of major health issues, some of the most serious of which being cancer, stroke, heart disease, and seizures.

There are many different and individual motivations for wanting to give up smoking. When confronted with a serious health problem or other life-or-death circumstance, the decision to quit smoking for good is made by many smokers. As smoking is responsible for more than 400,000 deaths annually in the United States, medical concerns are a typical impetus for quitting. Heart disease, cancer, and vascular accidents are the three diseases and conditions that result most frequently from smoking. In addition, smoking might make it more difficult to address preexisting illnesses, and it can also increase the risks of anesthetic and postoperative complications.

One more significant factor to consider is the influence of other people. Tobacco usage is now often regarded as offensive, sickening, and revolting, and smokers may have the impression that their peers do not accept them. Some people want to stop smoking so that they may set a good example for their children, while others want to demonstrate to themselves and to others that they are capable of exercising the self-control and intelligence necessary to kick the habit.

Another significant factor is the financial burden that comes with smoking. Many people who smoke are aware that they spend thousands of dollars each year on cigarettes, and the financial burden associated with this habit can be crushing. In addition, smoking can ruin clothing, autos, furniture, and carpets, and it can also result in expensive burns and unintentional fires.

Quitting smoking might be a challenging endeavor for some cigarette users. They might have attempted to quit in the past but were unable to do so, or they might believe that they do not have the self-control necessary to stop smoking. However, it is essential to keep in mind that smoking is an addiction, and that once one develops a dependence on a substance, they will always be considered an addict. To successfully quit smoking, you must make the decision to never pick up a cigarette again, and it is imperative that you are aware that even one cigarette can quickly turn into a full-blown addiction.

It is possible to quit smoking with the assistance of a number of different approaches, such as nicotine replacement therapy, behavioral therapy, medication prescribed by a doctor, and support groups. Finding the appropriate approach and formulating a strategy before making the decision to stop smoking can significantly boost the likelihood of success. In addition to this, it is essential to have a support system in place, whether that support comes from friends, family, or a professional in the medical field. It is important to keep in mind that quitting smoking is a process that demands patience and determination, but the rewards for your health and well-being will make the effort more than worthwhile.

Alterations To One's Way Of Life In Order To Facilitate Quitting

Modifying key aspects of one's lifestyle can be a huge help in the process of giving up smoking and can significantly boost one's chances of being successful in the long run. These adjustments center on the creation of a more healthy environment and the formation of routines that are beneficial to one's health in general. Changing the following aspects of your lifestyle may be helpful in kicking the habit of smoking:

1. Stay Away From Your Triggers Recognize what causes you to be tempted to smoke and stay away from those situations. This may involve avoiding locations in which smoking is common or decreasing the amount of

time spent in close proximity to those who smoke. It may also include making adjustments to one's regular routines, such as staying away from areas that allow smoking during breaks or discovering other activities that can take the place of smoking breaks.

2. Surround Yourself with Support: Create a solid support network consisting of friends, family, or support groups that are encouraging of your struggle to quit smoking and can understand what you are going through. Share with them your intention to kick the habit and solicit their help, as well as their moral and emotional support. Having people around you who believe in you and are able to help you get through difficult times may make a huge difference.

3. Make physical exercise a regular part of your life. Not only can regular physical activity help you forget about your desires, but it also improves your health in general. Regular exercise, such walking, jogging, or cycling, can help reduce stress, boost mood, and encourage the release of endorphins, which are natural mood enhancers. These benefits can be achieved by engaging in physical activity. Find things to do that you take pleasure in doing and make them a consistent part of your day.

4. Participate in Techniques for the Management of Stress Considering that quitting smoking can be a stressful process, the successful management of stress is essential to success. Investigate several methods of stress management to see which ones work best for you. Some examples of these methods include practicing deep breathing, meditating,

practicing yoga, or participating in hobbies or activities that help you relax. Try out a variety of approaches until you find one that enables you to relax and better manage the effects of stress on your life.

5. Work on Improving Your Diet Having a diet that is well-rounded and rich in nutrients can both contribute to your general health and assist you in quitting smoking. The consumption of a wide variety of fruits, vegetables, whole grains, lean meats, and healthy fats should be your primary focus. Caffeine and alcohol in large amounts should be avoided because they can stimulate cravings. Additionally, it is essential to consume sufficient amounts of water throughout the day in order to maintain adequate hydration levels.

6. Ensure You Get adequate Rest: Make it a top priority to ensure you get adequate rest and create a consistent schedule for when you sleep. Getting enough sleep is important for your general health since it improves mood, lessens irritation and weariness, and makes it easier to deal with stress and cravings. Develop a soothing pattern for winding down before bed, make sure you have a comfortable place to sleep, and make getting between seven and eight hours of great sleep each night your daily objective.

Find Healthy Ways to Manage Emotions
7. Find Healthy Ways to Manage Emotions Smoking is frequently used as a coping method for dealing with various feelings. Investigate other, potentially more beneficial methods of dealing with your feelings, such as keeping a journal, speaking to a sympathetic friend or

member of your family, consulting a trained counselor, or indulging in creative activities like making art or playing music.

8. Give yourself rewards, and celebrate the milestones and accomplishments you've reached along the way to quitting smoking. When you accomplish a particular objective, you should congratulate yourself by treating yourself to a favorite dinner, a night at the movies, or a new piece of equipment connected to your passion. Your determination to stop smoking might be strengthened by participating in activities that provide positive reinforcement.

Keep in mind that the goal of making these adjustments in your life is to assist you in quitting smoking and to ensure that you never pick up the habit again.

Because every person is different, you should try out a variety of approaches to determine which one is most successful for you. Your chances of successfully quitting smoking can be increased even more by combining the aforementioned lifestyle adjustments with additional smoking cessation methods, such as medication or counseling. Maintain your commitment, be patient with yourself, and congratulate yourself on each baby step you take toward a lifestyle that is healthy and does not include smoking.

Strategies For Physical Withdrawal Are Presented In An Attempt To Help Users Kick Their Habits

The Benefits and Drawbacks of Nicotine Replacement Therapies

Nicotine replacement therapies, often known as NRTs, are helpful tools that may be of assistance to you on your quest to give up smoking. These therapies deliver carefully calibrated quantities of nicotine to aid in the management of withdrawal symptoms and cravings, so making the process of quitting smoking easier to handle. NRTs, however, are not without their share of benefits and drawbacks, just like any other method. If you are able to weigh the benefits of each option against their drawbacks, you will be in a better position to decide whether or not to include them in your plan to quit smoking.

The following are some advantages of nicotine replacement therapies:

NRTs provide a continuous, controlled amount of nicotine, which can alleviate withdrawal symptoms such as irritability, cravings, and difficulty concentrating on tasks. 1. Reduced Withdrawal Symptoms: NRTs deliver a consistent, controlled dose of nicotine.

2. Gradual Reduction: Nicotine replacement therapies (NRTs) provide you the ability to progressively lower the amount of nicotine you take in, which makes the process of quitting smoking much more doable.

3.Improved Chances of Success Research has shown that the use of nicotine replacement therapies (NRTs) can considerably improve the odds of successfully quitting smoking, particularly when used in conjunction with behavioral therapy.

4. Provides a Structured Approach to stopping: Nicotine replacement therapies (NRTs) provide a structured approach to stopping smoking by providing a clear plan to adhere to and decreasing the uncertainty associated with quitting smoking cold turkey.

5. A Wide Range of Availability Nicotine replacement therapies (NRTs) are available in a number of different formulations, such as patches, gum, lozenges, nasal sprays, and inhalers. This gives you the freedom to select the approach that is most suitable for your preferences as well as your way of life.

Negative Aspects of Nicotine Substitute Therapies:

1. Nicotine Dependence: Using nicotine replacement therapy (NRT) can keep you at the same level of nicotine dependence as before. Even if the doses are regulated and much lower than what one would get from smoking, there is still a possibility of developing a habit of nicotine use.

2. Expense: Noninvasive respiratory treatments (NRTs) might rack up an expensive bill over time, particularly if they are utilized for a prolonged period of time. Despite this, it's possible that the overall cost will be less than what it takes to maintain a smoking habit.

3.Adverse Reactions: Nicotine replacement therapies (NRTs) may cause adverse reactions in some people, including nausea, dizziness, headaches, or skin irritation.

4. Difficulties During the Transition Making the switch from cigarettes to NRTs could require some time for adjustment. Altering both the delivery mechanism and the schedule could initially present some difficulties.

5. Psychological Dependence: It's possible that nicotine replacement therapies don't address the psychological side of smoking, which can involve habits, routines, and triggers that have nothing to do with nicotine.

Combining non-pharmacological treatments (NRTs) with behavioral strategies:

Consider combining non-invasive respiratory treatments (NRTs) with behavioral methods in order to make the most of the benefits of NRTs while mitigating the negative effects of their limitations:

Cognitive Behavioral Therapy (CBT): Behavioral interventions like CBT can help you address the psychological aspects of smoking by breaking the relationship between triggers and the need for nicotine. CBT can also help you address the physiological aspects of smoking by reducing cravings.

skills of Mindfulness and Stress Management Instead of relying exclusively on nicotine to cope with triggers and cravings, try incorporating skills of mindfulness and stress management into your daily routine.

Plan for Gradual Decrease: If you decide to take nicotine replacement therapy (NRT), you should create a plan for gradually decreasing the amount of nicotine you consume until you are able to quit using it altogether.

Signs And Symptoms Of Withdrawal

When a smoker stops, they frequently experience the following withdrawal symptoms: difficulty falling asleep, restlessness, irritability or unhappy feelings, depression, anxiety, and cravings or desires to smoke. (Centres for Disease Control & Prevention, Source Credit).

It does not imply that you will experience every common symptom or anyone in particular. I meticulously used that strategy when I was quitting. Since the strategy simply reduces chemical consumption by 10% every three days, it effectively treated all withdrawal symptoms.

Therefore, the body adapts to the lack of these compounds, and I had none of the withdrawal symptoms listed above.

From day one to day 28, everything was how it always was. Every day was regular after the full cessation, which occurred on day 28 and continued for more than 15 years, free from any withdrawal symptoms.

The only issue I had was that, after all these years, my appetite returned and I could eat healthily. As a result, I gained some weight at first, but I was able to keep it off with exercise. As far as managing your weight is concerned, stick to your BMI (body mass index). It is an added benefit if you are skinny (as measured by your BMI) and you are gaining weight as a result of stopping smoking, isn't that right?

Additionally, I would advise seeking medical assistance from a doctor if you are experiencing any withdrawal symptoms that are out of your control.

Using nicotine gum, patches, and vaporizers:

When quitting abruptly on a set date, nicotine gums and patches are typically advised. You may need to take supplements for short-term nicotine if you smoke 10–20 cigarettes a day and decide to quit all of them at once on that one fixed day.

This method does not involve vaping, nicotine patches, or nicotine gums because it involves a gradual withdrawal from the habit, one cigarette at a time, every three days.

I didn't use any nicotine gum or patches during this voyage because the technique taught my body and mind to function without nicotine. Therefore, since there was no need, I didn't need one. Since I didn't utilize any, I am unable to suggest that to you.

What Makes You Wish To Give Up Smoking?

If you've ever been to a coaching call, therapy session, or event, you're definitely accustomed to being asked "why?" This is due to the fact that every action you take is motivated.

There's a reason you started smoking. Additionally, you need a motivation for stopping smoking.

No matter how long you've smoked, one of the scariest and occasionally traumatic experiences for smokers is stopping. Because how can you consciously let go of that euphoric feeling completely? In the same way?

Let me share a brief tale with you.

A acquaintance of mine declared a few years ago that he was going to give up smoking for good. He answered questions on why he started smoking and why he wanted to stop after some prodding.

He immediately pictured himself living alone with his dad and his two younger siblings when his mother passed away. Therefore, nothing had prepared him for a new mother or for an outsider who may divert his father's focus from him and his brothers. He left home because he couldn't bear the thought of taking his beautiful mother's place. There, he made some new friends and started smoking.

"FAMILY," to put it simply, led him wrong.

Interestingly, his motivation for quitting smoking is "FAMILY." "I want to be with them again, spend time with them, and show them how much I love them," he remarked with a melancholy smile. I know they won't object if I keep smoking, but if I keep going in this direction, I fear they'll lose me before they know it." Even though I could hardly hear him, I could tell he was sorry for the time he had missed.

Stages exist throughout life. Remorse is an enormous reward if you have little control over what you say and do. Smoking meets the same end.

There are numerous health advantages to quitting smoking, some of which you may already be aware of, such improved heart and lung health. These advantages are just rational, which makes sense in a lot of ways. But, I've discovered that some folks have sentimental and occasionally charitable motivations for quitting, and they don't give a damn about the health advantages. Unbelievable, I know.

These days, the choice to stop smoking is totally personal, and every smoker has one or more motivations. These are a few of the reasons people give up smoking, based on my observations and conversations with others. Some might also apply to you.

You don't want to endanger other people.

suffer you observed that nonsmokers either go somewhere else or suffer a coughing attack whenever you smoke anywhere near them? If you haven't noticed, you've either been paying attention or you've been quite picky about where you smoke. Just so you know, that response is what your body, heart, and lungs experience every time you light up.

Secondhand smoke refers to any exposure to the smoke particles that you exhale. And like you, a lot of smokers actually detest the impression that smoking gives others—health-wise, not popularity-wise.

This is connected to the death of a well-known singer. He had never lit a stick in his life, yet smoke exposure was the cause of his death. One life lost as a result of the actions of another.

The smoke that enters your lungs as you exhale is known as second-hand smoke. They run the danger of developing heart, lung, and respiratory conditions as well as asthma from this.

Once you give up, the toxins from your smoke will no longer be inhaled by your loved ones, friends, neighbors, or family.

to become aware of and in charge of

Stability is mostly dependent on mindfulness, which also provides you authority over your life at any given time. You become aware of every event and impending action when you practice mindfulness.

It's possible for smoking to be a reflex action, particularly for addicts. Some find that the more they give in to the want to smoke, the less control they have over other seemingly unconnected choices, such as impulsive purchases, thoughtless remarks, and occasionally more severe actions like crossing the street recklessly on a busy road. When you ask, they explain that it's because it thrills and gives them goosebumps, making them feel good.

Few people can genuinely link their impulsive behavior to smoking, but those who do are willing to break free from the behavior once they recognize its powerful influence. You can only go above and beyond that by "awakening the mindful you."

People want to give up smoking because they want to feel conscious and in charge of their health. Being mindful prevents you from acting in an unethical way before you do. I promise you, it's a powerful Why. It might be your why.

Your bodily system isn't working well.

Studies have indicated that smoking damages blood cells and nerves, which results in various bodily problems.

When they realize that smoking is preventing their bodies from mending correctly because it isn't getting enough blood flow, some people decide to give up. Occasionally, the problem goes beyond inadequate healing and involves challenges with breathing, walking, or executing certain everyday activities.

Creating A Robust Support Network

Creating a strong support network is essential to stopping smoking and living a happy non-smoking life. Your success may be greatly impacted by the accountability, understanding, and support that your support system offers. This chapter will address the importance of community services and support groups, as well as the role that social support plays in helping people successfully quit smoking. It will also offer ways for getting family, friends, and loved ones to assist with quitting.

A. How Social Support Helps People Quit Smoking Successfully

Social support is essential for people to effectively stop smoking. Having people who care about your objectives and well-being can help you stay motivated, encourage you, and give you the direction you need when things become tough. Studies have indicated that smokers who have a strong support network are more likely to succeed in quitting than those who attempt to do it alone.

People who know about your experience quitting smoking can be a source of emotional support, encouragement, and accountability. Their confidence in your ability to give up and their comprehension of the difficulties you could encounter can be very helpful sources of inspiration and fortitude. Furthermore, social support can give a sense of belonging and lessen feelings of isolation. By making connections with people who are going through comparable circumstances, you can take solace in the knowledge that you are not alonc in your quest to live a happy, smoke-free life.

B. Techniques for Getting Help from Friends, Family, and Loved Ones

One of the most effective ways to increase your chances of successfully quitting smoking is to get the support of your loved ones. The following are some ideas for include your loved ones, family, and friends in your efforts to stop smoking:

Honest and transparent communication Tell your loved ones why you have decided to give up smoking and why this is so important. While you listen to their ideas and worries, express your wants and expectations. Establishing an atmosphere of support can be achieved through encouraging open communication.

Teach them how to stop: Assist those close to you in comprehending the difficulties involved in giving up smoking and the possible withdrawal symptoms. Please let them know how they can help you on your trip most effectively.

Ask for their support and responsibility: Inform your loved ones that your success depends on their support and responsibility. Request that they uphold your pledge to them and offer encouragement as you proceed.

Ask them to help you establish a smoke-free environment: Invite your loved ones to help you maintain a smoke-free lifestyle by not smoking in your company and by getting rid of any items connected to smoking from your house. Reducing triggers and temptations by creating a smoke-free environment can help a lot.

Plan non-smoking-related activities: Talk on anything other than smoking with your loved ones. Take part in outdoor activities, discover new interests, or plan activities that promote wellbeing as a group. You fortify your relationship and make memories free from smoking by concentrating on shared experiences that advance health and wellbeing.

Celebrate achievements as a group: When you hit big milestones in your quitting journey, celebrate them with the people you love. Whether it has been a week, a month, or a year since you gave up, acknowledge your accomplishments and how they have improved your life. Their joy and encouragement will strengthen your resolve to stay smoke-free.

C. Looking into Local Resources and Support Groups for Added Help

Community resources and support groups can provide extra help on your quit-smoking journey, in addition to the support of your loved ones. Think about the following choices:

Local services or programs to assist people in quitting smoking: Look for community-based programs or services. These programs frequently offer access to resources that can help your efforts, therapy, and support groups.

Internet support communities: Look through social media pages, online discussion boards, and websites dedicated to quitting smoking. These online groups provide a forum for interacting with people on like paths, exchanging stories, and gaining knowledge and guidance.

Professional support services: You might want to think about getting assistance from medical specialists who specialize in helping people quit smoking, like physicians, therapists, or counselors. They can create customized quit programs, offer expert support throughout your quitting journey, and offer individualized guidance.

Support groups: Attending or starting an online or in-person support group can provide you a sense of community and support from people who are trying to give up smoking. In a group context, sharing your experiences, setbacks, and victories can inspire, advise, and motivate you.

You may increase the size of your support system and gain insight from the experiences and collective knowledge of people who have been through similar struggles to stop smoking by looking into these community resources and support groups.

The practical methods for maintaining long-term success and avoiding relapse will be covered in the upcoming chapter. You'll leave this chapter with the knowledge and attitude needed to continue living a smoke-free life and look forward to a healthier future.

Recognizing The Connection Between Smoking And Reducing Stress

One practice that has been widely linked to stress relief is smoking. For numerous smokers, the act of smoking a cigarette might offer a moment of serenity and relaxation, aiding them in managing the obstacles of everyday existence. Smoking is actually a substantial cause to stress and anxiety, despite the common belief that it relieves stress. This chapter will look at the relationship between stress and smoking, explaining why people who smoke use cigarettes to cope with their feelings and why it's ultimately a bad habit.

The effects of nicotine, the addictive ingredient in tobacco, are the reason why smoking is viewed as a stress reliever. Nicotine quickly enters the brain of a smoker through inhalation, causing a pleasurable and calming sensation. This is commonly known as a "nicotine buzz," and depending on the dosage, it may linger for a few minutes or longer. Part of what makes smoking addicting is the pleasure that comes with the habit; this is also the reason why some smokers use cigarettes as a coping mechanism for stress and worry.

But the effects of nicotine wear off quickly, and smoking itself can raise stress levels over time. Nicotine is a stimulant that can elevate blood pressure, quicken heartbeat, and induce jitters and anxiety. Furthermore, smoking can exacerbate stress and exhaustion by altering sleep patterns and lowering the quality of sleep.

Smoking also causes stress in the environment and in society. Smoking has well-known detrimental effects on one's health, like as lung cancer and heart disease, and it may also be extremely stressful and anxious. Furthermore, smoking is frequently linked to discrimination and social stigma, which can cause emotions of loneliness and humiliation. Many smokers find that quitting can be an arduous and unpleasant process, which exacerbates their stress levels.

In conclusion, despite the common belief that smoking relieves stress, the habit actually has a significant role in the development of stress and anxiety. Short-term nicotine effects are common, and smoking can eventually raise stress levels.

Finding healthy and productive coping mechanisms, such as exercise, meditation, or other stress-reduction methods, is essential to managing stress. In addition to lowering stress levels, quitting smoking can enhance general health and wellbeing. Smokers can escape the vicious cycle of stress and smoking and discover a better, more satisfying life with the correct help and tools.

Exploring The Addictive Nature Of Nicotine

First of all, The fundamental cause of the smoking habit is nicotine addiction. It's critical to comprehend nicotine's addictive properties if you want to successfully stop smoking. This chapter will examine the science underlying nicotine addiction, its physiological and psychological impacts, and how understanding this information can help you overcome the obstacles associated with quitting smoking.

Section 1: The Science Behind Addiction to Nicotine

1.1 The Brain's Reaction to Nicotine

Nicotine is a potent psychoactive drug that modifies the reward system in the brain. Nicotine enters your bloodstream quickly when you smoke or use tobacco products, and it takes only a few seconds for it to reach your brain. After entering the brain, nicotine attaches to nicotine receptors, which causes the release of dopamine and other neurotransmitters that are involved in reward and pleasure perception. It becomes harder to stop smoking because of this cycle of reliance that is created by the reinforcing impact.

1.2 The Addiction Cycle

Addiction to nicotine has a cyclical structure. Smoking causes the nicotine breathed to attach to nicotine receptors, which causes a dopamine spike and a pleasurable feeling. But the effects of nicotine wear off quickly, and as your body's nicotine levels drop, cravings start to surface. You are forced to smoke again by these cravings, which feeds the addiction cycle.

Section 2: Nicotine's Effects on the Body and Mind

2.1 Nicotine's Physical Effects

Your body's organs and systems are impacted by nicotine. Cardiovascular issues result from vasoconstriction, which narrows blood vessels and lowers blood flow. Nicotine further stresses the cardiovascular system by raising blood pressure and heart rate. It also has an impact on the respiratory system, which raises the risk of lung diseases and causes respiratory problems. Recognizing the damage nicotine causes to your body requires an understanding of its physical effects.

2.2 Nicotine's Psychological Effects

Nicotine's addictive qualities are partly attributed to its profound psychological impacts. It can briefly reduce tension and anxiety and increase focus and attention span as well as cognitive function. As a result, smoking and the intended outcomes become psychologically associated, which causes a conditioned response that strengthens the smoking habit. To overcome nicotine's psychological hold on you, you must acknowledge its influence.

Section 3: The Dependency on Nicotine and Its Withdrawal

3.1 Addiction to Nicotine

As you smoke continuously, your body becomes physically dependent on nicotine. Your brain becomes accustomed to nicotine with time, requiring bigger dosages to provide the same effects. Because of this tolerance, one needs more nicotine, which feeds the addiction even more. Cravings, withdrawal symptoms, and an intense want to smoke are signs of nicotine dependency.

3.2 Rehab Signs and Symptoms

As your body becomes used to not having nicotine, you could encounter a variety of withdrawal symptoms when trying to stop smoking. Anger, restlessness, impatience, difficulty concentrating, increased appetite, and sleep difficulties are some examples of these symptoms. Knowing that these symptoms are only momentary and a normal aspect of stopping will help you find the willpower and determination to keep going.

In summary:

The strong addiction to nicotine sits at the root of the smoking habit. A successful quit smoking journey requires an understanding of the science underlying nicotine addiction, the physical and psychological effects of nicotine on the body and mind, and the difficulties associated with withdrawal from nicotine. With this information at your disposal, you may approach quitting smoking with a sense of resolve, confident that you can conquer your addiction to nicotine and start living a better, smoke-free life. We'll look at natural approaches and techniques in the next chapters to help you overcome your addiction to nicotine and successfully stop smoking.

Sustaining An Alcohol-Free Lifestyle

After quitting smoking, it's critical to concentrate on keeping up your smoke-free lifestyle. We'll talk about tactics for maintaining your success and adopting a healthier lifestyle in this chapter.

Create new habits and routines.

You may avoid slipping back into old patterns and help yourself detach from your past smoking life by forming new routines and habits.

Create a wholesome morning schedule: Start your day off right with a healthy breakfast, then work out, practice meditation, or engage in other activities that help you create a positive outlook for the day.

In place of smoke breaks, If you used to take smoke breaks during work or other everyday activities, try substituting healthier activities like stretching, taking a stroll, or sipping tea.

Make fresh social customs: If you used to smoke after dinner or at parties, try new activities, games, or conversation starters as alternative ways to unwind and mingle.

Effectively handle stress

Developing healthy coping strategies to handle stress without smoking is essential because stress can be a major trigger for relapse.

Engage in mindful meditation: By increasing your awareness of your thoughts, feelings, and physical experiences, mindfulness can help you better control your stress levels and cravings.

Make use of relaxing methods: Guided visualization, progressive muscle relaxation, and deep breathing are techniques that can help reduce stress and foster calm.

Put self-care first: Make time for the things that make you happy and relaxed, including hobbies, time spent in nature, or treating yourself to a spa day or massage.

bolster your network of supporters

Having a solid support system is essential to keeping up your smoke-free lifestyle. To share your experiences and get support, keep interacting with friends, family, and support groups.

Continually show up to support group meetings: Attending support group meetings can offer continuous encouragement and assistance in overcoming obstacles related to upholding a smoke-free lifestyle even after you have quit.

Get in touch with people online: Engage in social media groups, internet forums, or applications created specifically to assist those who have given up smoking.

Help others on their path to quitting: Talk about your experiences and give advice to people who are attempting to give up smoking. Giving back to the community can strengthen your resolve and inspire you to keep up your smoke-free lifestyle.

Honor your accomplishments.

Celebrating and recognizing your successes can help you stay committed to quitting smoking.

Create benchmarks: Decide on benchmarks to commemorate, such quitting smoking for a month, six months, or a year. Celebrate these accomplishments with a fun activity or little gift.

Consider your development: Examine how your health, money, and general well-being have improved since you stopped smoking on a regular basis. This might act as a potent reminder of the advantages of leading a smoke-free life.

Tell us about your achievements: Celebrate your advancements and let your support system know about your accomplishments.

In summary, it takes constant dedication, self-awareness, and support to sustain a smoke-free lifestyle. You may maintain your smoke-free lifestyle and take advantage of all the advantages it offers by creating new routines and habits, learning effective stress management techniques, building your support system, and acknowledging your accomplishments. Accept your new, healthier lifestyle and keep developing and thriving as you go on your path to better health.

SYMPTOMS OF ABSTINENCE

Nicotine, especially from smoking, stimulates the body and mind in a similar way to heroin or cocaine. Nicotine has detrimental impacts on both the physical and psychological aspects of the body. As such, the very notion of quitting smoking is mentally taxing. One will definitely feel motivated to press on rather than quit up as a result. Furthermore, it is hard to resist the unwanted and inevitable pressure from friends and colleagues. You become aware of your future only if you possess the strength to resist getting dragged into a relationship this intense. Thus, we recommend that you first be convinced of the advantages of giving up smoking. We have to admit that making the decision to persevere or give up requires commitment.

These symbols

It is possible to faint during the initial days. You'll also experience fatigue and discomfort. This is the outcome of not smoking a specific amount of cigarettes at a very specific time of day.

● Depression: The allure of nicotine lies in its ability to elevate your emotional state. ● Impatience and Fury – Nicotine affects the blood vessels, brain, hormone system, metabolism, and lungs in addition to the lungs. As a result, the consequences of withdrawal could upset your entire body, which would increase mental strain in a world where stress, tension, and intense rivalry are your regular companions.

● Sleeping and Concentrating: This is a reaction to many disorders of the hormone system. Since your mind needs to be in harmony to focus on any work that demands your complete concentration and to have a good night's sleep, you feel as though there is a loss of harmony.

● Digestion and Appetite: The doctors observed unexpected outcomes after quitting smoking, including altered appetite and digestion. Research has indicated that sometimes the stress of quitting smoking results in dyspepsia. In a few rare cases, the withdrawal symptoms from nicotine have directly affected metabolism, causing an increase in appetite.

Why Is It So Hard For Me To Stop Smoking?

Josh, who was my initial mention, asks this question all the time. I wonder whether I should have to tell you why he continued and how he is going to quit doing this going forward.

It is challenging to stop smoking for a variety of reasons, some of which are covered below:

● Physical Cigarettes: Nicotine is a medication that, when inhaled, produces the brain chemical dopamine to arrive, which gives you encouragement. Unfortunately, as the dopamine wears off, the smoker experiences a craving for more cigarettes as a result of these sensations returning. Along with a physical dependence and nicotine tolerance, smokers need to smoke more to get the same effects. The FDA has approved seven drugs that can help with these symptoms when trying to stop smoking. Speak with a medical expert to find out more about your choices.

● Mental smoking occurs regularly in day-to-day interactions. When in a given emotion, like tension or fatigue, or during specific times of the day, like while driving or sipping coffee, smokers are more inclined to light up. Smoking can become a hindrance, similar to a trustworthy companion. Remain focused on quitting by identifying these moments and triggers, retraining yourself or altering your behavior to key areas of strength, and continuing to be a desire.

● Social Several smokers from social groups that revolve around smoking take their friends or coworkers out for a smoke break. You can also use the query "Got a light?" as a way to start a conversation. Similar to this, depending on social networks that encourage quitting can be beneficial. According to a recent survey, 80% of smokers said that getting support from friends, family, partners, and coworkers is very important for quitting successfully. Rather of quitting on the spur of the moment, tell your trusted pals about your decision. You need their assistance, we assure you.

You'll be surprised to learn that Josh's pregnant wife smokes as well. I was taken aback when he revealed that to me. My mind went to what would happen to the unborn child. Many addicted pregnant smokers have questioned why it's so difficult for them to give up. In the following chapter, let's examine the reasons why quitting smoking while pregnant is difficult and how to overcome it.

Locating Help And Encouragement Along Your Path To Quitting

Making the important choice to quit smoking is a huge decision that calls for determination, commitment, and support from loved ones and friends. Even though quitting smoking is an entirely personal decision, having a solid support system can make all the difference in the world in terms of how successful you are. When you are in the most need of encouragement, direction, understanding, and accountability, support can supply all of these things for you. This is the power that support possesses. In this introductory essay, we will investigate the significance of obtaining assistance during the process of quitting smoking and talk about the various types of support that are available to assist you in realizing your objective of stopping smoking for good.

1. Emotional Support: Quitting smoking can bring on a wide range of feelings, including anxiety, irritation, cravings, and self-doubt. Having someone there to support you through these feelings can be very helpful. Emotional help from friends, family, or support groups can provide a secure environment for you to share your experiences and feelings in an open and honest manner. They have the ability to lend an ear, empathize with your situation, and reassure you, all while serving as a reminder that you are not the only one going through this challenge. When you're going through tough times, it might be helpful to surround yourself with people who understand the difficulties you're going through. This can help improve your morale and keep you motivated.

2. Being Accountable: Keeping your resolve to give up smoking is significantly easier if you have someone to hold you accountable for your actions. When you tell other people about your plans to quit smoking, it gives you a sense of responsibility and makes it more likely that you will keep those plans. Pick a reliable friend, member of your family, or support group who can help you take responsibility for your behavior and provide you with gentle reminders when they are required. Your accountability partner can provide the extra push you need to get through setbacks and keep going when you check in with them on a regular basis or update them on your progress.

3. Seek the Assistance of a specialist Seeking the assistance of a specialist will significantly boost your chances of successfully stopping smoking. Professionals in the healthcare industry,

such as physicians, registered nurses, or counselors specializing in smoking cessation, are equipped with the knowledge and experience necessary to assist you with stopping smoking. They are able to provide individualized guidance, make suggestions for tactics supported by research, and deliver medical interventions when required. Having access to professional support increases the likelihood that you will receive correct information, tailored instruction, and a holistic strategy for quitting smoking.

4. Support Groups: Participating in a support group that is intended solely for persons who are attempting to kick the habit of smoking can be of great help. Individuals who are going through similar struggles might feel a sense of kinship and understanding among one another through participation in these organizations. Taking part in group

conversations, talking about personal experiences, and gleaning wisdom from the paths traveled by others are all excellent ways to get useful insights, coping skills, and moral support. A helpful and non-judgmental environment is created through support groups, providing participants with the opportunity to freely express themselves and draw strength from the group's collective commitment to give up smoking.

5. Participating in Online Communities
In this day and age of technology, participating in online communities and forums provides a support system that is both convenient and easy to access. Individuals are able to communicate with one another, share their experiences, and seek guidance through the use of a variety of internet platforms that give these opportunities. Participating in online groups where

individuals who have successfully stopped smoking or are going through the same experience as you are may share their stories, offer advice, and point you in the direction of useful resources is a great way to get the support, advice, and insights you need to kick the habit. However, due to the fact that not all sources may be genuine, you should exercise caution and verify the credibility of the information that is shared online.

6. Participating in Smoking Cessation Programs You should give some thought to participating in smoking cessation programs or workshops designed to assist persons on their path to quit smoking. These types of programs frequently mix educational aspects, behavioral therapy strategies, and the dynamics of support groups in order to provide a comprehensive approach to the process of quitting smoking. They provide structured assistance,

counseling, and resources to assist you in developing effective coping mechanisms, managing urges, and remaining abstinent over the long term. By providing you with the knowledge and skills essential to overcoming obstacles, smoking cessation programs have the potential to vastly improve your chances of being successful in your efforts to quit smoking.

7. Your close Circle of Family and Friends Your close circle of family and friends can be an extremely helpful source of support. If you tell your loved ones about your intention to quit smoking, they will be able to offer the support and understanding you require during this difficult time. Make an effort to enlist their help in eliminating smoking from your surroundings, avoiding situations that could stimulate your want to smoke, and discovering

new activities that you can enjoy together as a group. Their support, encouragement, and participation in your efforts to kick the habit can be quite helpful in ensuring your ultimate triumph.

It is important to keep in mind that seeking help while you are on your quest to stop smoking is not a sign of weakness but rather a testimonial to your strength and resolve to lead a life that is healthier. Accepting the assistance of others, whether it be in the form of emotional support, the direction of a trained professional, or participation in a support group, can considerably boost the likelihood that you will be able to effectively quit smoking. By cultivating a network of support for yourself, you can assure that you will always have a group of people who can empathize with your challenges, provide you with direction, and rejoice in your successes. If you have the correct support system in place, you will be able to discover the encouragement and the strength you require to triumph over obstacles and realize your objective of quitting smoking.

The Complete And Final List Of Excuses To Give Up On Something

There is no justification for you to feel ashamed about the fact that you are having difficulties stopping your habit. You should not feel guilty about this. Figuring out how to make changes in any element of your life is going to be difficult no matter what, but if you don't have the correct motivation behind it, it may be even more difficult to figure out how to make those changes. Because of this, it is essential to compile a list of the motives driving your decision to kick the habit of smoking. While you are going through this difficult time in your life, this will make it easier for you to maintain your motivation and hold yourself accountable to your goals.

In the meantime, I'll offer you with the definitive list of reasons to quit smoking. You are the only one who can decide which argument is more convincing than the other, but I'll give you those arguments anyhow. There are just as many beneficial reasons to stop smoking as there are beneficial reasons to keep doing it.

It is not always an easy process, but giving up anything that is bad to us has the potential to be the best decision we ever make in our life. If we give up something that is harmful to us, our lives will likely improve significantly. It's possible that you're having difficulties quitting smoking, or it's possible that you just can't seem to stop eating too much junk food despite the fact that you know it's bad for you. Either way, it's possible that you're having trouble quitting anything unhealthy. In either scenario, the desire to stop doing whatever it is that you're doing needs to be powerful enough to be able to prevail over the need to continue doing it. The following list of reasons to quit will help motivate you and give you the strength to finally cease doing whatever it is that is hindering you from being the best version of yourself. The list also includes reasons to quit smoking, drinking, and doing drugs.

This list of the top ten reasons to quit smoking was developed for the purpose of providing you with inspiration and motivation at a time when you may use it the most. It was only logical that we began with the most compelling reasons to stop the habit because there are so many positive reasons to kick the habit. The longer you keep smoking, the more damage you will do to your body, and the more difficult it will be for you to ultimately stop the habit once and for all! This exhaustive list of reasons to quit smoking includes not only the beneficial benefits that quitting will have on your physical health but also the positive impacts that quitting will have on your mental health. This is a thorough list of reasons to quit smoking. If you want to start living a better life, the first thing you should do is read this extensive list of reasons why you should stop smoking. This is the best place to start if you want to start living a healthier life.

It is a lot less difficult to give up something when all of the reasons to do so are right there in front of you, waiting to be accessed at the precise moment when you feel the need to do so the most. This list of reasons can be of assistance to you in breaking a bad habit, overcoming an obstacle, or simply deciding whether or not it is time to make a substantial alteration to the way that you live your life. Keep reading to find out what you need to do to quit doing whatever it is that you should stop doing as soon as possible and find out how to achieve it!

Quitting a bad habit, especially one that you've been partaking in for a significant amount of time, such as smoking, drinking, or participating in another harmful action, can be a tough endeavor.

This is especially true when the habit in question is one that you've been indulging in. Here is a complete list of reasons why you should quit smoking, which we have compiled so that you may continue to focus your attention on the beneficial benefits that quitting smoking will have on your attempts to enhance your overall health and wellness.

Whether it's giving up smoking, giving up drinking, or giving up their work, there are a lot of various elements that go into a person's decision to give up something that they formerly enjoyed doing and were excellent at, like a career or an activity. These causes may be broken down into two categories: external and internal. When faced with the potential of making such a difficult decision, it is only natural to experience anxiety; nonetheless, there are occasions when doing so is necessary for the sake of the greater picture. This list of the ultimate reasons to quit will guide you through the usual worries and anxieties that people have when trying to make this decision in their own life, which will help you make your decision by guiding you through these fears and anxieties. [Citation needed] This list of the ultimate reasons to quit will help guide you through the common fears and anxieties that people have when trying to make this decision in their own life.

It cannot be stated in a plain manner. It is imperative that you step down from your position as quickly as possible. Now is the moment, not tomorrow, not next week, and most definitely not in two months when the semester will be done; rather, the time to act is right now. You are aware, on some level, that it is not functioning properly; nevertheless, you have not been able to acknowledge this to either yourself or others owing to the worry that you feel around the implications of coming clean. You have not been able to acknowledge this because you have been unable to acknowledge that it is not functioning properly.

Putting down the cigarette, putting down the drink, and putting down the fast food are all fantastic examples of things that you can do to improve the quality of your life as well as your general health. But when you're trying to decide if giving up something will be worth it in the end, it might be beneficial to look at it from as many perspectives as possible in order to obtain a thorough picture of the issue. This includes considering the experiences of other people who have quit the same thing as you have in the past. This list gives seven various reasons why other people have stopped smoking, drinking, or eating junk food, along with tips and insights from those people on what it was like to quit, how much better they feel now that they have stopped, and how difficult it was to quit in the first place.

Quitting smoking or any other bad habit may seem impossible, but in truth, it is much easier than you might imagine it would be. Have a look at this list of reasons why you should give up, and then do some research on how to maintain your drive as you get closer and closer to accomplishing your goal. It will take some work on your part to rid yourself of bad habits, but in the long run, doing so will make you a happier and healthier person.

Quitting smoking is one of the most difficult things you will ever have to do, but the benefits are more than enough to make it worthwhile to put in the effort. If you read the following list of reasons to quit smoking, not only will you be better prepared to quit smoking, but you will also be reminded of why quitting smoking was such a wonderful idea in the first place.

It is not as simple as you might think to make the decision to stop doing something, especially if you have been doing it for a big length of time or if it comprises a substantial piece of your life. If you have been doing it for a significant amount of time or if it constitutes a significant portion of your life, it is not as straightforward as you might think. There are always reasons to keep going, and rather than giving up totally, you would probably be better off looking for different methods to make the activity more fun rather than giving it up entirely. There are always reasons not to stop. On the other hand, there are some activities that simply aren't worth the investment of either your time or your money, and your life will go in a way that is much more manageable if you don't participate in them. Make use of this list as a help in considering whether or not to give something up, but keep in mind that your circumstances are unique from those of everyone else's!

The Arguments In Favor Of Quitting

In the United States, smoking is a significant problem that affects the public's health. A recent research from the Centers for Disease Control and Prevention found that more than 20% of adults in the United States smoke cigarettes, and of those individuals, more than 80% smoke cigarettes on a daily basis. An addiction to nicotine can result in a number of major health issues, some of the most serious of which being cancer, stroke, heart disease, and seizures.

There are many different and individual motivations for wanting to give up smoking. When confronted with a serious health problem or other life-or-death circumstance, the decision to quit smoking for good is made by many smokers. As smoking is responsible for more than 400,000 deaths annually in the United States, medical concerns are a typical impetus for quitting. Heart disease, cancer, and vascular accidents are the three diseases and conditions that result most frequently from smoking. In addition, smoking can make the treatment of preexisting problems more difficult, and it can also raise the risks of anesthetic and postoperative complications.

One further significant factor to consider is the influence of other people. Tobacco usage is now often regarded as offensive, sickening, and revolting, and smokers may have the impression that their peers do not accept them. Some people want to stop smoking so that they may set a good example for their children, while others want to show themselves and others that they are capable of having the self-control and intelligence necessary to stop smoking.

Another significant factor is the financial burden that comes with smoking. Many people who smoke are aware that they spend thousands of dollars each year on cigarettes, and the financial burden associated with this habit can be crushing. In addition, smoking can ruin clothing, autos, furniture, and carpets, and it can also result in expensive burns and unintentional fires.

Quitting smoking might be a challenging endeavor for some cigarette users. They might have tried to quit in the past but were unable to do so, or they might believe that they do not have the self-control necessary to stop smoking. However, it is essential to keep in mind that smoking is an addiction, and that once one develops a dependence on a substance, they will always be considered an addict. To successfully quit smoking, you must make the decision to never pick up a cigarette again, and it is imperative that you are aware that even one cigarette can quickly turn into a full-blown addiction.

It is possible to quit smoking with the assistance of a number of different approaches, such as nicotine replacement therapy, behavioral therapy, medication prescribed by a doctor, and support groups. Finding the appropriate approach and formulating a strategy before making the decision to stop smoking can significantly boost the likelihood of success. In addition to this, it is essential to have a support system in place, whether that support comes from friends, family, or a professional in the medical field. It is important to keep in mind that quitting smoking is a process that demands patience and determination, but the rewards that it will bring to your health and well-being are more than worth the trouble.

Step Three: Carry Out Your Investigations

You will now see how putting in a little bit of effort pays off in this situation. Keep in mind that the time you spend on this activity right now will serve you very well when the cut-off date finally comes around. Spend some time doing research about tobacco and smoking on the internet and at libraries to learn as much as you can about the subject. Learn more about the diseases that are associated with smoking. Find out how many people die each year from smoking-related illnesses, all of which are entirely preventable; how much money the NHS spends each year attempting to treat people who have these illnesses; again, all of which are entirely preventable; and the valuable resources that could be spent on other elements of healthcare. Learn more about the chemical and psychological addiction to tobacco, as well as the other health risks associated with smoking, such as heart disease, stroke, mouth and lung cancer, gum disease, and more. Find out how much of an improvement in your health you can anticipate after you have given up smoking for a day, a week, a month, a year, or even five years after you have quit smoking. Again, all of this information and research will slowly start to assist remove you mentally and emotionally from the addiction to tobacco. You will quickly discover that there are no benefits or positive sides to the habit of smoking, and you will also find out that there are no positive features to the behavior. Remember to keep this new information in mind while you go about your daily routine of smoking, drawing closer and closer to the date that you've marked on your calendar as the day you will quit. You should print out the pieces of information that particularly speak to you on a personal level. It could be an image, a statement, an illustration, a quote, a figure, a statistic, or some other fact. After you have successfully quit smoking, you will, if necessary, refer to the information contained in this "smoking pack."

As a step in this process, you should get started on creating little posters that you can hang throughout your house. These posters should contain powerful affirmations and positive sentiments; they are messages to yourself from yourself, to remind you how strong you are without cigarettes, and to remind you that cigarettes only serve to ruin your life in a highly detrimental way. A statement that may be used on a poster could read as follows: "you are a strong and powerful being, you no longer need these pitiful, small, white sticks, and you are no longer a drug addict." This is an example of a statement that could be used on a poster. Every day that you are able to stay away from this addiction, your health, money, and happiness will continue to improve and become more beautiful. Create many posters, each with a unique combination of images and/or text. Include in your response some of the material that was covered in the prior section, such as how much money you are saving every day and some significant facts on ailments that are caused by smoking. Make sure they are as powerful and passionate as you can make them. Put them in strategic locations throughout the house, such as in the kitchen, beside the bedside table, next to the sofa in the living room, even in the bathroom and on the back door. This will ensure that they are easily accessible at all times. If you find that you are having trouble protecting yourself, these are essentially your "back-up" or supplementary defense mechanisms. Again, they help to strengthen your mental fortitude and contribute to the process of gradually severing the links that bind you to your smoking habit. Remember to keep these posters in mind as you go about your daily business and to think about the previously mentioned statements every time you light up a cigarette, such as the fact that you will not be smoking for the rest of your life, that you will stop smoking in the near future, that you will think about the health research that you have done, and that you should imagine you are flushing a fifty pence piece down the drain every time you have a cigarette. At this stage in the journey, you may come to the realization that you are beginning to feel disgusted with the habit, that every time you smoke a cigarette you now feel as though it tastes bad, and you find yourself wondering why you are even bothering to try to quit in the first place. In the event that this occurs, it is important to acknowledge these sensations, recognize that they are really the unconscious results of all of your laborious work, and proceed with the strategy as outlined below.

It is time to let all of your loved ones, friends, and coworkers know that you are going to quit smoking, and now is the perfect opportunity to do it. It is impossible to overstate how helpful it is to have the support of one's family and friends throughout this endeavor, which at times can be challenging. Receiving supportive phone calls and encouraging texts is very helpful. However, if any of your other friends are smokers, it is vital that they take your efforts seriously and do not try to dissuade you from taking this beneficial step. It is in your best interest to quit smoking. If they do not choose to support you, that is their prerogative; but, they have no right to get in the way of your efforts to live a better life (and may be acting this way out of a fear of abandonment, considering that you are abandoning a sinking ship, etc.). Continue doing what you're doing and keep your strength up in spite of the adversity.

At this point, some of you may believe that everything being discussed is completely unnecessary and excessive. That is not in the least bit problematic. Recognize that it is completely unnecessary, but carry it out nevertheless. You can then pass this advice on to another smoker, confident in the knowledge that you will have added years to your life and saved both yourself and the NHS a significant amount of cold, hard cash. Trust me, if you are serious about quitting smoking (which by now you will be), it will all be worth the effort. It is also important to note that the idea of giving up smoking is a great deal more frightening than the act of giving up smoking itself. If you give close attention to each and every one of the directions provided in this article, you will be able to give up smoking with only a moderate degree of difficulty.

There Are Numerous Varieties Of Smoking Products

It is essential to keep in mind that all forms of tobacco usage are hazardous to one's health and might lead to unfavorable outcomes. Putting an end to your use of cigarettes or any other form of tobacco can have numerous positive effects on both your health and your financial situation.

Cigarettes: Cigarettes are the most common form of smoked product and consist of tobacco that is wrapped in paper. Cigarettes are the most popular form of smoked product.

Cigars: Cigars are similar to cigarettes, but they are larger and are typically wrapped in a tobacco leaf instead of being individually wrapped.

Pipes: A bowl for the tobacco and a stem or mouthpiece are the two primary components that make up a pipe. Pipes are used for smoking.

The term "hookah" refers to a type of water pipe that is used for smoking flavored tobacco. A tobacco bowl, a stem, a hose, and a water chamber are the standard components that make up this accessory.

Electronic cigarettes, often known as vapes or vape pens, are battery-operated devices that vaporize a liquid mixture that typically contains nicotine along with a variety of other man-made chemicals.

Tobacco products that don't require lighting up, such as snuff and chewing tobacco, are used by placing the tobacco product in the mouth or nose rather than smoking it.

QUIT SMOKING FOR THE SAKE OF YOUR HEALTH: LUNG CANCER

Cancers are a pain in the... anyplace you want to put it. There are carcinomas in your respiratory tract if you have lung cancer. These carcinomas are generated by the dead cells that refuse to leave the body. And even if there have been a lot of developments in science and medicine that have made it possible to cure it recently, the results are still leaving a lot to be desired. But in the meantime, we continue to work.

When treating lung cancer, radiation therapy is frequently utilized as a treatment modality. In what is more often referred to as radiotherapy, high-energy radiation is used in an effort to kill cancer cells. The effect that it has is not always a negative one; nevertheless, not every patient responds to it in the same manner that others do. Have the doctor examine you first so you can have a better understanding of the intricacies of your individual condition.

There are some cases in which the attending physician may correctly surmise that there is a greater risk associated with eliminating the tumors of your lung cancer than there is with allowing them to remain. When something of this like does take place, though, you will likely have no choice but to pay attention to what they have to say. I understand that this can't be an easy decision for you, but you should submit to the surgeon's expertise in this matter.

As a potential side effect of several lung cancer treatments, you can experience flushing of the skin at times. This occurs as a consequence of constriction in the blood vessels. Other potential adverse effects include hair loss, puritis, itching, desquamation, sloughing off of the outer skin layers, and other similar phenomena. The list of benefits is much longer than the length of my arm, but the most important benefit is that you recover from the cancer that would have caused your death. There does not appear to be much of a selection available to you there.

Treatment for lung cancer can cause side effects such as pain, atrophy, and shrinkage, as well as enhanced pigmentation; edema and swelling; and of course, damage to the developing fetus. Radiotherapy, a treatment method that has been available for some time, is responsible for the majority of these side effects. Alternatives are being looked for and discovered, but not all of them are as effective as the technique, so it continues to be used.

Thoracoscopy, also known as the video assisted thoracic surgery (VAT), is a relatively new method that has been shown to be quite beneficial in the treatment of lung cancer. Because it is less intrusive than some of the other options, a lot of patients choose to go with this one instead of the others.

Maybe you should give it some thought as well.

For the treatment of lung cancer, a video-assisted thoracoscopy, also known as a VAT, is less invasive than a thoracotomy but does not provide as much information as the latter. It does not truly make it possible to perform a comprehensive examination of the lungs in order to locate and remove any metastases that were not seen on the preoperative chest X-ray. If the doctor intends to use that on you, you will be required to give your full consent before they can proceed; otherwise, it's game over. You have grasped it.

There are several stages of lung cancer, each of which plays a role in determining the potential treatment options available. You have the option of undergoing a straightforward lobectomy if the disease has not yet progressed too far, or you could opt to have your lymph nodes removed instead. Do not be alarmed by the names; all they really mean is that the tumor will need to be removed.

Some of the methods that are used to treat a condition actually pose a greater risk to a patient's life than the condition itself. I mean, I have no idea what the physician would say about this, but if I had to choose between taking my chances or letting someone cut me up over lung cancer, I would choose to take my chances. On the other hand, you can have a different opinion.

If you have lung cancer that is judged inoperable by a surgeon, they may recommend photodynamic therapy as an alternative treatment option for you. It is a treatment in which a light-activated drug is injected into your system before an examination of your airways using a flexible scope. The process begins with the administration of the drug. Now that they can see the tumor, they can make an attempt to remove it using laser light after they have done so.

Stopping smoking right away is the most important step you can take to ensure that you will not have to go through any of these problems in the future.

Words Have Power: How Hypnotic Suggestions Can Change Habits [The Power Of Words]

Have you ever given serious consideration to the power that words hold? How can something as basic as a sentence cause such a torrent of feelings or cause a shift in our perspective on anything? Imagine, then, how words that have been thoughtfully selected and organized could modify your habits and free you from the grip of tobacco addiction. In this chapter, we will discuss the power of hypnotic suggestions and how they can be the key to unlocking your success in quitting smoking. Specifically, we will look at how these suggestions can help you break the habit of smoking.

Why is it critical to have an understanding of the function that words play in hypnosis? Now, suggestions made under hypnosis form the cornerstone of hypnotic therapy. When you are under the influence of hypnosis, certain words and concepts are implanted in your subconscious mind to take the place of the unhelpful thoughts and beliefs that are preventing you from quitting smoking. However, not every word has the same significance. Some are more effective than others, and the way you utilize them can make all the difference in your journey toward a life free of tobacco dependence.

First, before we get into the subject of hypnotic suggestions, I want you to take a time to think about your life. Which phrases or expressions have made a major impression on you? What key phrases have motivated you to make significant decisions or caused you to shift your perspective? We can begin to comprehend how hypnotic suggestions can be transformative aids in our process of quitting smoking if we first acknowledge the power that words have in our everyday lives.

Let's take a look at the interesting realm of hypnotic suggestions and the ways in which they can change your smoking behaviors as well as your ideas about smoking. In the following sections of this chapter, we will discuss the main research and concepts underlying hypnotic suggestions, and you will understand how carefully picked and structured words can be your best ally in the fight against tobacco addiction. In the next section, we will discuss the key research and concepts behind hypnotic suggestions.

So what is it about certain words that gives them greater power than others? The explanation can be found in how our brain analyzes these words and how they relate to the most fundamental aspects of our beliefs, values, and feelings. Robert Cialdini is a social psychologist and an authority on the psychology of persuasion. In his book "Influence: The Psychology of Persuasion" (1984), he emphasizes the significance of utilizing words and ideas that are congruent with our internal needs and aspirations. When we do this, we increase the likelihood that we would agree with a proposal and permit it to have an effect on our behavior.

When it comes to quitting smoking with the help of hypnosis, one of the most effective strategies is making suggestions that target the psychological as well as the physiological components of tobacco addiction. For instance, phrases that bring to mind thoughts of health and well-being, such as "breathe deeply" and "renewed energy," can be very beneficial. Similarly, ideas that reinforce the sense that smoking is unwanted and harmful, such as "cigarette smoke is repulsive" and "cigarettes poison my body," may be useful in modifying views and attitudes toward smoking. For example, "cigarette smoke is repulsive" and "cigarettes poison my body."

In addition to choosing the appropriate language, it is essential to ensure that the ideas have the appropriate structure and tone. Joseph Kappas, a clinical psychologist and hypnosis expert, wrote the book "Hypnosis and Suggestion in the Treatment of Smoking" in 2001. In this book, he emphasizes the significance of employing positive, future-focused suggestions rather than negative, fear-based recommendations. It is hypothesized that if a person quits smoking and concentrates on the positive ways in which their life will change as a result of the change, they will be more intrinsically motivated to make the change and will have a greater chance of being successful in the long run.

For instance, rather than saying, "If you continue to smoke, you will have serious health problems," a more productive recommendation would be to state, "By quitting smoking, your health will improve, and you can enjoy a longer and happier life." It is more probable that the individual will accept the recommendation and put it into practice if the change is presented in a manner that is more appealing to the eye and emotionally resonant.

It is imperative that you immerse yourself in the process of consciously and freely receiving these ideas now that you are aware of the power of words and how to pick and arrange excellent hypnotic suggestions. In the following section, we will discuss specific examples of hypnotic suggestions that have been successful in helping smokers quit smoking, as well as how you might implement these techniques in your own life to stop smoking.

www.ingramcontent.com/pod-product-compliance
Lightning Source LLC
Chambersburg PA
CBHW050417120526
44590CB00015B/1993